COOKING WITH CLIFFORD

Cooking with
CLIFFORD
New Irish Cooking

MICHAEL CLIFFORD

MERCIER PRESS

Mercier Press
PO Box 5, 5 French Church Street, Cork
24 Lower Abbey Street, Dublin 1

© Michael Clifford 1993

ISBN 1 85635 070 3

Illustrations: John Sheehan Photography Ltd., Adelaide Street, Cork.

A CIP for this book is available from the British Library

Printed in Ireland by Colour Books Ltd.

SPONSORS

AIB, 67 Patrick Street, Cork
Carbery Meats, Clonakilty, Cork
Coral Seafoods Ltd., Watercourse Road, Cork
Cork Bar and Catering and Supplies Ltd., Cork
CMP Dairies, Kinsale Road, Cork
ESB, Wilton, Cork
Fyffes Group Ltd., Beresford Street, Dublin
Jamaica Banana Co. Ltd., Togher, Cork
K. O'Connell Fish, Grand Parade, Cork
John O'Flynn and Sons Ltd., Marlboro Street, Cork
Pat Tiernan Family Butcher, Dublin Hill, Cork
Tom Whelan (Veal), 'Stormydowns', Windsor Hill, Glounthaune, Cork

Acknowlegdements

*Thank you to Deirdre, my wife, and our two
beautiful children – Peter and Laura
To Liam and Betty whose help and kindness I will
never forget
To Brendan and Catherine, Paddy and Laura for
all their help
To all my friends and customers – a big thank you
for all their support.*

Contents

Vegetables 71

Desserts 77

Breads 85

Glossary 93

Foreword

I first met Michael Clifford when he was head-chef in White's on the Green in Dublin, slim, pink-cheeked, silver blond, and looking like a junior chorister from St Patrick's Cathedral. He must have a sinister Dorian Gray-style portrait upstairs on whose face all the hassle of chefdom is imprinted, for nine years later he looks perhaps six months older.

One of my proudest boasts when he was in White's was, that on occasion, I ate in the kitchen there. Beat that for style! But one of the great experiences of my life occurred in the regular dining-room after the customers had left. Michael had bought a sturgeon, twenty-six pounds of prehistoric monster with horny circles along its flanks like pot holes, dragon ridges on its back, and an astonished O for its mouth ... it cost £1,456. Peter White was surprised and interested on his return from a London trip to find himself the owner of this *Jurassic Park* stand-in. He and Michael invited me and a couple of others to lunch on it after service in the restaurant had finished for the afternoon.

We inspected the body laid out in the kitchen, paled a little, and then retired for fortifying drinks while the feast was preparing. We ate it in three luxurious courses, each of sturgeon cooked in a different way. First came sturgeon in a sauce of champagne and sorrel; this was followed by thin slices of raw sturgeon with horseradish, Japanese sashimi style; to finish we had hot smoked sturgeon. Each was incomparably delicious. I worked out the cost, based on the residual weight when the armour-plating and the guts were removed. Merciful hour! The raw materials alone of my snack lunch came to £75. I thought guiltily for a minute, of Cleopatra and the pearl dissolved in vinegar which she gave to Mark Anthony as a cocktail. The guilt lasted only a minute, for then came the glow in the stomach and the realisation that we had made several fishermen very happy indeed.

There were other great memories of long late lunches and dinners ending at dawn, surrounded at other tables by the glittering stomachs of Dublin eating-out society. Apart from the sturgeon there were milestone dishes such as a dozen oysters each cooked with a different sauce, or the spiced beef with mango, or a divine little soup with fairy parcels of ravioli in it. There was also the status of being seen with not only the utterly charming proprietors at my table, but that stunning chef as well. (It is always a pleasure to see rival ladies gnash their teeth.) White's on the Green was one of the great restaurants of my life.

Tears trickled down my face when Michael left for Cork. I followed him to Washington Street to sample his goodies, and then to the Mardyke. It would suit me just fine if he opened a sub-office in Dublin. Failing that, his book of recipes will be my standby.

Helen Lucy Burke

Introduction

Cork is a lucky place for restaurants. We have the mildest of climates, a multitude of small local suppliers who hand-raise their produce, a sea filled with the choicest fish, and restaurant customers who have travelled widely, and have lost their prejudices about food. Furthermore, food now has an important position; people not only eat food, they talk about it too.

For me, the most important thing about food is freshness first of all, and then how one makes use of that freshness. I don't believe in messing with food, such as combining too many ingredients just for the sake of doing it. It's fashionable, but it can result in food which tastes of nothing in particular. My strong opinion is that food should taste of its ingredients. Good stock is a basic of my cooking, and I want my chicken stock to taste of chicken, and the same with beef, veal or fish stock. If you add something to the stock such as tomatoes, they too should have a discernible flavour.

The great Escoffier said it all when he said, 'Faites simple'. Or almost all, for I would amplify; make it simple and use the very best ingredients you can get of their kind. This could mean a superbly made black pudding, an elegant crúibín, or a neck of the tenderest young lamb – or at another level, the fattest freshest liver of a Strasbourg goose.

In Cork old walled gardens hold treasures unobtainable elsewhere in Ireland. The owners come to me in early spring with baskets of greeny-white seakale, one of the most delicious vegetables you can eat, and enormously popular in Victorian days; it is virtually unknown now on our tables though it grows wild around our coasts. There are eggs from special breeds of hens, some like mops with plumes all over their faces, some with breeches of feathers down to the ground; all of them scratch their food out by themselves from the seeds and insects in those gardens.

Later the baskets will contain tiny wood-strawberries whose sharp intensity of flavour has never been reproduced by commercial growers, and raspberries untouched by chemicals, and the spiked heads of artichokes, which are a kind of thistle and grow as freely here as their villainous cousins. The plump purple figs which come my way in autumn are grown in only two of these gardens, but given a sunny wall could be grown by anyone.

I weep to think how we under-use our resources. Apart from that seakale, samphire grows abundantly in river estuaries and is never eaten. I cooked it when I was a chef in Holland, and that wild plant commanded an enormous price. (In youth samphire resembles French beans poking up from the mud. Later in life it gets spiky, and when cooked looks like a small boiled Christmas tree. Quite, quite delicious.) We recognise only field mushrooms, while fungi that the Continentals would eat are left to rot.

With our soft rainy climate, Ireland is singled out by nature to be the country of the snail, and snails, I am happy to say, are becoming a standard item with my customers who have travelled in France. Our locally bred ones are big and juicy crying out for a bit of garlic butter. Squid, shark, sea-urchins – people now tackle them fearlessly on the plate, but still demand fish with the head removed (except, oddly, for cold salmon in a buffet where they seem quite pleased to share a smile with him). I notice too that people are still a bit glum about meat which is cooked rare.

Knowledge and appreciation of food starts in the home, and unfortunately our tradition of food is very cautious and conservative. Interesting ingredients are not widely known though, as I have said earlier, they can be grown here with the utmost ease. Our best native ingredients are seasonal – but I believe in seasonal cooking. I'm not a freezer person, though I admit it has its place. Neither am I an import person, but until oranges, lemons, bananas and passion-fruit grow here I have to conform.

My meat suppliers are some of the best in the world. Small butchers have a day-to-day knowledge of their product, and a love for it and a pride in it which ensures quality. My part is to see that it is properly aged, by hanging it in my own cold-room. And of course I make sure I have offal to put on the menu every day. Offal is badly under-used in Ireland, although it tastes marvellous and provides essential elements for health: captive lions all round the world failed to breed until Dublin zoo found that for fertility they needed the innards as well as the muscle meat. My fish comes from West Cork, often from men with one trawler, fished by themselves. As for game – much of it falls to my own gun. And game is not just expensive pheasant shooting. Many farmers will welcome you with open arms if you shoot the marauding woodpigeons for them: and you will have the makings of a soup which would grace a king's table.

Butter has been an Irish traditional ingredient from Stone Age times. And as many dietitians reverse themselves on the subject of what is healthy every two years, I follow my gut-instinct that nothing so delicious could be harmful in moderation, and I continue to use it where it is appropriate, such as for pastry where its flavour is incomparable, and unmatched by any margarine.

Traditional local ingredients, combined with know-how picked up in various countries – that forms the cooking that I have aimed at during my cooking career.

As a small boy I never wanted to own a guitar and sing Rhythm and Blues. I never wanted to line out for Manchester United. I never wanted to be Taoiseach. I wanted to cook. And I wanted this as far back as I can remember. Semolina pudding and rock-buns were my strong points, when I was the only boy in the school taking Domestic Economy (my voluntary choice) alongside nine girls. Small boys are not discriminating eaters being more like human disposal units; I scoffed the semolina and even the tapioca, but my favourite treat then was toast cut thick and spread with good beef dripping. The jellied meat juices seeped through into the soft centre and liquified pleasantly against the tongue: to this day I am ready to put in a good word for my favourite.

As an adolescent, Pavlova cake burst on my astonished palate. Again the contrast of textures seized me. Crisp outside, chewy and toffeeish inside, cream in soft clouds topping the fragrant freshness of raspberries picked in the garden while the sun still warmed them. Surely making this miracle was the occupation of a demigod? (Adolescents are wolfish: I remember demolishing half of that party-piece, nearly the size on an ice-floe.)

Exactly eight summers after my first reverent bite of Pavlova I was in Paris, living in a sort of cupboard with a washbasin and a view of the Champs Elysées from six storeys up. My job was commis chef aboard the good ship *Peniche Ile de France,* a ship which never left port for it was really a stationary restaurant – very prestigious – moored opposite the Eiffel Tower. We in the kitchen knew when boats were passing by the way our copper saucepans rattled in their wash, but ne'er a boat saw we; the kitchen was twelve feet below the surface of the river Seine, and ran the length of the boat.

It was a hell-hole of organised chaos which served a hundred guests at lunch, and maybe a hundred and fifty at dinner. The work was hard, the pay was miniscule, and we often worked from eight in the morning until midnight under the glare of the tough Basque chef. I was on the sauce station. (Professional kitchens are divided into as many as six stations, usually meat, vegetables, cold larder, pastry and sauces, with a *chef de partie* in charge of each.) Did that mean I could relax once I had reduced my fish stocks to an ambrosial essence and produced a Bechamel like white velvet? It most emphatically did not. My superiors urged me towards other stations with kindly admonitions if they saw me with a spare second. The cooking was of the old elaborate style with every vegetable 'turned' by hand to an exact evenness of size and shape. Many a morning after making a vat apiece of eight basic sauces, I 'turned' a thousand potatoes with a knife that moved in a blur of light.

France with its passion for cooking perfection had been a revelation. Second best was never allowed to pass. I haunted the markets where the salads came in from the countryside, each leaf crisp and unblemished as if designed to sit on a plate in a costly restaurant. There were fruits of which I had never heard, and which have still to reach Ireland. At home, grapes had been a sort of acid tonic, black or green, brought in to a sick person in hospital; on their native soil they burst from their skins with as many flavours as apples used to have in Ireland. There were long oval muscatels with a taste of elderflowers, and little dark ones which tasted of strawberries. Apricots did not live in tins, but were laid reverently in single layers in baskets. Fish with sinuous bodies and cynical expressions, the kind that I have seen heaved off Irish trawlers into the sea, changed hands at enormous prices and were turned into meals of unsurpassed delicacy.

The great and famous dish at the *Peniche* was seabass stuffed with herbs and grilled, but we apprentices did not get to eat it. Instead we fed on earthy but delicious meals of tripe and black-pudding and bits of intestine so rude that I had never dreamed they could be eaten. These we cooked ourselves in between feeding the paying multitudes. The greatest revelation was, that most of the food could be grown in Ireland without the slightest difficulty. Where were *our* goose markets? Where were *our* specially bred long-bodied ducks? And the white turnip that went with these ducks in a superb marriage were used as tender pink-flushed babies, not the coarse woody monsters which featured on most Irish tables.

In Cork and Kerry I had seen the pike caught by the anglers hurled back into the water as a mere nuisance: pike which the French housewives turned into the ambrosial feather-light *quenelles de brochet* for which gourmets would kill. I learned the glories of perch and carp, sold at markets for tidy sums, and at home given to the cat. (By the way, the trick with perch is to skin them in boiling water before cooking, in the same way you skin a tomato.) You only had to know how to get the best out of each fish, and this seemed inborn in the thrifty French housewife whose sons and daughters were brought up with none of the squeamishness towards unfamiliar food which was native to us. Oh yes, at that time we still had chickens in Ireland which tasted of chicken, but the battery rot had set in and the cheap and cruel and nasty-tasting process soon established its supremacy.

France has chickens with yellowish flesh which had been fed on corn, and white-fleshed capons as plump as turkeys, and eggs with deep orange yolks and tough shells as befitted eggs whose mothers had foraged for their own food. At home snails were a pest to be stamped on: French snails were valued, and were hunted in a ritual that resembled the mushrooming or blackberrying of my childhood. The Burgundian type even dressed better than Irish snails, in a handsomely striped cream jacket. And these free-range snails are subjected to a reverent ritual of starving, rinsing, cleaning and bathing in garlic butter before being served to an appreciative table in specially designed dishes which gave them the same dignity as oysters. Furthermore, so valued were free-range snails that they were actually getting scarce, and being talked of as an endangered species, something incomprehensible to a country lad from Kerry.

To be young in Paris was enough, even when my pockets were empty, though I managed to moonlight in cafés on Sundays. During any free afternoon I attended French classes, or went around the museums and art galleries. Fauchon's in the Place Madeleine was a place of magic where I learned the reverence that is due to food. The assistants handled each individual fruit or vegetable with the tenderness of nurses towards babies so that nothing blemished appeared on the shelves, no bruises developed after they were sold. And the scent of the tropical strangers, mangoes, guavas, durians, passion-fruits, wafted out the door on the breeze and mingled with the smells of coffee and pastry from the Fauchon branch across the street creating a magic that engaged all the senses.

This can be done in Ireland, I thought, and I want to do it. I want my own restaurant. I want to search out local suppliers of fresh Irish raw materials, and I want to cook with them food of the standard we cooked on the *Peniche*.

After my semolina and rock-bun days in the domestic economy class, a family friend suggested Rockwell Catering College. It was the Eton College of the catering industry, and gave a first class training. Unfortunately the majority of the students came completely raw, as there was no great tradition in Ireland of family restaurants run by successive generations who knew the life, and accepted it. Quite a lot of students dropped out during training.

When I finished my training my ambition burgeoned: nothing but the best was going to be my motto from then on, and instead of applying to a variety of lesser establishments I made a single application – to the legendary Claridge's in London. I was accepted, and while waiting for a place there I cooked for the Jesuits in farm street, a place equally legendary in a different way. It was not at all as Evelyn Waugh had suggested in some of his novels. Far from living flamboyantly the good fathers ate such ordinary fare as roast beef and cabbage, or bacon and cabbage, and were unexacting employers. It was not the kind of cuisine to challenge an impatient young chef, but I cooked the bacon with all the skill I possessed, and made sure the cabbage was crisp and juicy, for even the simplest meal can be transformed when the ingredients are treated with respect and love. I still have the reference they gave me when I left, praising my time-keeping as well as my industry.

Royalty used Claridge's as their second home. Diplomats negotiated there, and film stars of the richer and soberer kind took suites there for months at a time. Anyone who got work there was privileged, but we staff were kept strictly to our own quarters, and never even heard the names of the guests, far less saw them. Instead, our stars and our royalty were the temperamental chefs whom I saw in action for the first time. Copper-pots provided standard flash-points. The crash of pots hurled against walls, while not a daily matter, was usual enough to raise no comment. We trainees kept our heads down, and did whatever we were told. Rockwell College had taught me basic skills, but somehow, there in rural Tipperary, uniformity of potatoes had not seemed a vital matter. I was to learn my error.

I dreamed one morning of Cork and that Pavlova as I sculpted a potato to shape. Suddenly a muscular hand seized the nape of my neck while the other hand thrust a turned potato within an inch of my nose. 'Do you call that a potato?' intoned a furious voice. The unfortunate vegetable still looked like a basic potato with lumpy sides, instead of becoming a thing of sculpted oval beauty. It was made plain to me that I was far from being a demigod. Unless the vegetables were a uniform size and shape they cooked at different rates, quite apart from not having the svelte haunches which looked good on a plate, and the chef was right – but that was not surprising. A standard French kitchen saying begins 'Le chef a raison' – the chef is right, and goes on to say, 'the chef is always right. even when the chef is not right, he is right', and it was something you did not forget with that chef.

Paris and Lancaster Hotel followed, and the *Peniche* came next. Then came a spell in Amsterdam at the famous Ciel Bleu Restaurant in the Hotel Okura as a sauce chef; this was a significant step upwards in the kitchen hierarchy. Nouvelle Cuisine was the fad or fashion of this time, lightness very much emphasised which meant learning a completely different sauce technique. As the Okura was Japanese owned and run I also learned the traditional art of ice carving from the Japanese chefs.

My next position was in the new de Kersentuin restaurant also in Amsterdam. This restaurant was not long in becoming one of Holland's finest, receiving the coveted Michelin star. It was a real temple of nouvelle cuisine, a technique of cooking which has left a valuable legacy behind it, of lightness and freshness. To the de Kersentuin came the top chefs of the world, who came to visit and demonstrate their culinary skills. Any time off I had was spent getting further work experience with such demigods as the brothers Troisgros (Roanne, France), Roux Brothers in London and the Waterside in England, the Bonne Auberge in Antibes (south of France), Le Chapon Fin in Thoissey near Lyons, the Laurent in Paris – Champ Elysées.

Wild Geese have itchy wings, but in the end every Wild Goose longs to fly back home, rest the wings, and put hard-won experience to good use in one's own private nest. After my return I worked in several restaurants before I took up a position as head-chef in Whites on the Green, a restaurant which established for itself a standard of excellence. I was recruited by Mr Peter White and his wife Alicia, given a free hand to design my own kitchen, and let get on with my own ideas of what New Irish Cooking should be. It was a very happy time in my life. The Whites were ideal employers. I met customers who became friends that I still know and value. And I met my wife Deirdre. But every chef wants his own restaurant. I found it in Cork, in a run-down premises in Washington Street (my architect and my interior designer changed all that!) and soon the little restaurant bulged at the seams with the pressure of customers.

Eventually I flapped a hundred yards up the road, turned a couple of corners into the Mardyke with its dilapidated County Library, which I purchased, renovated into a luxurious nest and there I folded my wings. Come and visit me.

Michael Clifford

Sauces and Stocks

Most chefs if pressed admit that sauces are their greatest interest, and I am no exception. A sauce can raise a dish from the good to the supreme; unfortunately the great sauces always demand a good stock base. Yes, stock-making is a tedious and long-boiling process but the point is, stock can be trusted to simmer away on its own and you need not sit with it. During a beef stock's three to four hour simmering time you can wash the car and paper a room. Fish stock is the loner among stocks with a very short simmering time, and if you overstep it, you get a saucepan of fish-glue. Remember a good stock's role in cooking vegetables, when it can turn the humble potato into a duke.

Apart from the time taken, the drawbacks are the fuel-cost, and the expense of the ingredients extra to the main dish which the sauce is intended to enhance. With granny's cooking back in vogue, there is a case for resurrecting some of granny's thriftiness, such as using a hay-box for long simmering which can be trusted never to overboil. Besides, many butchers and fishmongers give away bones and pieces which can go into the stockpot. However as a professional chef I must warn you that it is a daunting experience to fill a twenty gallon pot with expensive ingredients, and see them reduce down to something that would fit into a cough bottle.

If after these words of encouragement you still do not want to embark on this haute cuisine standby, remember that there is plenty going for a nice sauce of melted butter. We are told that margarine has many wonderful qualities, which it employs beavering away in the arteries, but in my opinion it has no place in a sauce.

Fish Stock

Ingredients

50g fennel, finely sliced
50g leek, sliced
50g onions, sliced
50g unsalted butter
900g fish bones
120ml dry white wine
1$^{1}/_{2}$ litres water
3 slices of lemon
3 sprigs of parsley
sprig of tarragon
6 black peppercorns

Method: sweat the vegetables in the butter over moderate heat until they are soft but not coloured. Add the fish bones and cook for a further 1 minute. Add cold water and wine and bring back to the boil. Skim off any impurities. Add the lemon slices, herbs and black peppercorns and simmer for a further 20 minutes. Pass through a sieve.

Chicken Stock

Ingredients

1 kilo of chicken carcass preferably raw (including wings and bones but make sure to trim off any excess fat)
2 litres of water
1 bunch of herbs, tied
2 small carrots
1 large onion
6 crushed peppercorns
2 cloves

Method: put cold water into a deep saucepan with the bones and chicken carcass. Bring to the boil and skim off any excess fat. Wash, peel and chop the vegetables and add to the stock with the tied herbs, peppercorns and cloves. Simmer for 1¹/₂ hours skimming constantly. Pass through a sieve. Keep any excess stock in a covered bowl in the fridge.

Basic Beef Stock

Ingredients

2kg beef bones
5 litres of water
500g roughly chopped vegetables
1 bunch of tied mixed herbs
6 cloves of garlic
100g mushroom trimmings
2 tomatoes, chopped
1 bottle of cooking red wine

Method: trim all fat off the bones. Brown well in hot oven. Put bones in stock pot and fill with water. Bring to the boil and skim. Brown vegetables in pan and add to stock. Add tomatoes and mushroom trimmings. Also add tied herbs. Simmer for 3–4 hours, skimming constantly. In a separate pot, reduce the red wine by half its volume and then add to the reduced stock.

Note: when using brown stocks for sauces reduce gently to required sauce consistency.

Basic Lamb Stock

Ingredients

2kg lamb bones
5 litres of water
500g roughly chopped vegetables
1 bunch of tied mixed herbs
6 cloves of garlic
25g tomato purée

Method: same as beef stock (see page 28). (Spread tomato purée onto bones before putting them in the oven.)

Note: veal and pork stock is made in the same way as the lamb stock but by using the appropriate bones instead.

Basic Brown Game Stock

Ingredients

500g game bones (duck, pigeon, rabbit or pheasant, preferably raw)
1 litre water
100g roughly chopped vegetables
1 bunch of tied mixed herbs
1 tablespoon of tomato purée
2 cloves of garlic
6 juniper berries
6 peppercorns
1 glass of red wine

Method: trim and chop the bones. Spread with tomato purée. Place in hot oven with vegetables. Add garlic and brown well. Put into pot, add red wine, water, juniper berries, peppercorns and bunch of tied mixed herbs. Bring to boil, skim and simmer for 2–3 hours, replacing water if necessary. Strain and cool.

Basic Lemon Butter Sauce

Ingredients

50ml white wine
1 tablespoon of white wine vinegar
1 tablespoon of lemon juice
150g unsalted butter (cut into cubes)
1 shallot finely diced
2 tablespoons of cream
6 peppercorns (white)
Seasoning to taste

Method: put shallots into pan. Add vinegar, reduce slightly. Add lemon juice, white wine and peppercorns. Reduce until a syrupy consistency is achieved. Add cream with 2–3 drops of cold water. Reboil and remove from heat. Gradually whisk in cold butter and return to gentle heat for 1 or 2 minutes. Season and correct consistency. Pass through a fine sieve. Keep in a warm area until required.

Note: this is a basic lemon butter sauce and can be adapted for use either with meat, fish or vegetable dishes by adding various fresh herbs, wines or champagnes.

Basic Fish Cream Sauce

Ingredients

250ml fish stock
150ml white wine
1 shallot finely diced
1 teaspoon of white wine vinegar
500ml cream
Seasoning to taste
1 knob of butter

Method: sweat the shallot in the knob of butter. Add the white wine and the vinegar and reduce by half. Add the fish stock and then reduce to a syrupy consistency. Add cream and then reduce to achieve a light consistency. Season and pass through a fine sieve.

Note: this is a very adaptable sauce and has many uses. Again, you can add herbs, vermouth or champagnes to make it more luxurious.

Vinaigrette Dressing

In Italy they say that a day without a salad is like a day without sun. That pretty well disposes of any chance of a sunny Irish day, for salads we are not strong on. I don't mean a ritual slice of flavourless tomato and a lettuce leaf beside a steak, to fill the bare space. My idea of a salad is a bountiful bowl containing crisp leaves and shoots and stalks and flowers, forming a kaleidoscope of colour, texture and taste. At a minimum you should have three different kinds of leaves which have been carefully washed and thoroughly dried. (If you leave water on the leaves the dressing simply rolls to the bottom of the bowl.) Each crisp leaf should glisten with a vinaigrette made from the best quality oils; no skimping, for a stale oil or an inferior oil will merely ruin the dish. My Vinaigrette Dressing has been developed over the years to give a constant excellent result.

yields ¹/₂ litre

Ingredients

125ml white wine vinegar
125ml virgin olive oil
125ml hazelnut oil
125ml vegetable oil
1 teaspoon of lemon juice
1 sprig of fresh thyme and rosemary
1 clove of garlic
12 white peppercorns
1 teaspoon of sea salt

Method: put herbs, garlic, salt and pepper into a storage jar. Combine all the liquids and pour into the jar.

Note: it is important to use good quality oils and vinegars to get the best results. Shake the jar well before serving.

Starters

Poached Free Range Egg on a Bed of Spinach Served with Nuts and Grapes

I admit that children traditionally hate their greens, and I also admit that a brutally heaped plate of soggy boiled cabbage would test any nose or stomach and could put children off greens for life. But try them with my dish of Poached Egg (free range!) on a Bed of Spinach, served with Nuts and Grapes. Indeed, try it on anyone. The contrasts of flavour and texture are brilliant, and of course eggs and spinach are, since time immemorial, a marriage made in Heaven.

serves 4

Ingredients

**250g fresh spinach
4 free range eggs
50g of assorted roasted nuts, ie, cashew, pine-kernels, hazelnuts or peanuts
20 green grapes (halved and deseeded)
Seasoning
Pinch of nutmeg
2 tablespoons of olive oil
100ml reduced chicken stock (see page 27)
1 tablespoon of port
25g butter**

Method: poach eggs to desired point. Heat olive oil in large pan and add spinach leaves. Toss constantly until tender. Season with salt, pepper and nutmeg. Put reduced chicken stock into a small pot. Add the nuts and the grapes, boil and reduce slightly. Add port and whisk in butter. To assemble dish, place spinach in the centre of the plate. Place the egg on top and pour the sauce neatly around.

Note: this dish can be varied by using a butter sauce. See page 31.

Ogen Melon with Smoked Beef Scented with Sauternes and Passion-Fruit

serves 2

Ingredients

**1 ripe ogen melon
6 thin slices of smoked beef
1 passion fruit
Sauternes to moisten
Freshly milled black pepper**

Method: finely slice the melon. Arrange neatly around the plate. Place smoked beef in the centre of the plate. Garnish with passion-fruit seeds and pulp, then sprinkle with sauternes and milled black pepper.

Note: make sure that the melon is ripe. This is a simple recipe and takes very little time to prepare.

Roast Quail with Asparagus Mousse

serves 4

Ingredients

4 quail
8 asparagus spears (peeled and uncooked)
1 egg
2 egg yolks
250ml cream
1 teaspoon of lemon juice
1 clove of garlic
1 knob of butter
Olive oil
Seasoning: Salt, freshly ground black pepper, pinch of nutmeg

Method: purée asparagus spears in food processor and gradually add egg and egg yolks. Add cream. Season well with nutmeg and lemon juice. Pour into 4 buttered ramekins and cook in a bain marie for 6 minutes. Prepare quail and season. Place in hot roasting pan with some butter, olive oil and the garlic for 10–12 minutes. Cook at 180°C. Then assemble.

Note: a nice sauce can be made by using the bones of the quail and cooking juices and flavoured with walnut oil. Irish asparagus when available should be used.

A Warm Smoked Haddock Salad

Smoked fish used to be eaten in Ireland as a Lenten penance – but it is a wonderful raw material, fit for gourmets. Do not imagine that Gourmet Smoked Fish means only salmon. Good Smoked Haddock (by which I mean the genuinely smoked fish, not the artificially dyed horror) is as great a delicacy in a heartier and cheaper way. My Smoked Fish Terrine (see page 43) uses expensive ingredients, and will win you acclaim; for comfort eating among friends you will find yourself returning again and again to the Warm Smoked Haddock Salad.

serves 4

Ingredients

500g smoked haddock
50ml virgin olive oil
Juice of 1/2 lemon
2 tablespoons of dill, chopped
Freshly milled black pepper
Assortment of crisp salad leaves
Vinaigrette dressing (see page 33)

Method: arrange finely sliced smoked haddock on a large plate. Mix olive oil and lemon juice and brush lightly on the smoked haddock. Sprinkle on dill and milled pepper and place under the grill or in the oven for 3–4 minutes. Toss salad leaves with the vinaigrette dressing. Place haddock in centre of the plate and arrange salad leaves around the fish. Serve immediately.

Note: this is a very refreshing and delicious salad, particularly in the summer.

Shrimp and Lentil Soup

serves 6–8

Ingredients

500g fresh shrimps
1 small stick of celery
¹/₂ onion
¹/₂ leek
1 small carrot
1 tablespoon of tomato purée
100g green lentils (pre-soaked)
1 litre fish stock
250ml fresh cream
1 clove of garlic (finely diced)
1 bunch of herbs tied together
Salt and pepper to taste
1 tablespoon of olive oil

Method: chop the vegetables finely. In a hot pan, fry the shrimps and garlic in the olive oil. Add vegetables and tomato purée. Cook for two minutes. Add fish stock, lentils and herbs. Simmer for 30 minutes. When cooked, liquidise and pass through a fine sieve. Add cream and correct seasoning.

Note: for presentation, you could add some peeled shrimps to the soup.

Hot Chicken Liver Mousse

serves 6

Ingredients

100g chicken livers
300ml milk
2 whole eggs
2 egg yolks
¹/₂ clove of garlic crushed
Nutmeg
Dash of brandy
Seasoning

Method: trim chicken livers and then liquidise. Add remainder of ingredients and mix well. Season to taste. Rest for 1 hour in the fridge. Pour mixture into buttered ramekins and bake in a bain marie for 10–15 minutes. When cooked, make sure to loosen sides and turn out.

Note: a nice green peppercorn flavoured sauce would complement this mousse.

Crab Cakes Dusted with Fine Herbs

serves 4

Ingredients

500g potatoes (peeled)
200g cooked crab meat
2 tablespoons of Vermouth
1 shallot (finely diced)
Salt, milled pepper and pinch of paprika
50g fine breadcrumbs
25g finely chopped fresh herbs
1 knob of butter

Method: cook potatoes, drain and return to heat to dry out. Purée potatoes, add crab meat and season. In separate pan fry shallot in half of the butter. Add vermouth, potato and crab meat. Mould into cakes. Dust with breadcrumbs and herbs. Fry gently in a pan with remaining butter until brown and crispy.

Note: other fish may be substituted for the crab, ie, salmon, cod etc. Make sure that the potatoes are not overcooked.

Clifford's Smoked Fish Terrine

Ingredients

2 fillets of smoked trout *(make sure to*
2 fillets of smoked mackerel *remove any*
500g smoked salmon *small bones that*
100g smoked eel *may be in the*
4 hard boiled eggs finely chopped *smoked fish)*
25g chopped parsley
150ml fish jelly (clear fish stock with 2 leaves of gelatine)
Milled white pepper to taste

Method: line terrine with thinly sliced smoked salmon. Break up trout, mackerel and eel with your fingers. Layer fish neatly into terrine and alternate smoked fish and chopped egg and parsley. Pour on warm fish jelly. Cover with slices of smoked salmon and place in fridge until set – approximately 1 hour.

Note: this goes very well with a yoghurt dressing flavoured either with Pernod or fresh dill.

Celery and Apple Soup with Roasted Hazelnuts

yields 1¹/₂ litres

Ingredients

1 litre chicken stock (see page 27)
300g celery
75g leeks
75g onions
2 apples
30g butter
250ml fresh cream
1 medium potato (peeled and diced)
Lemon juice
Seasoning to taste
5oz crushed roasted hazelnuts
1 bunch of herbs tied together

Method: wash and finely slice vegetables. Peel and dice apples. Melt butter in pot, add vegetables excluding potato, cover and sweat for 5 minutes over a gentle heat. Add apple and cook for another 2 minutes. Add potato and chicken stock. Bring to the boil and skim. Add bunch of tied herbs and simmer for 15 minutes. Liquidise and pass through a fine sieve. Add cream, return to the boil and check seasoning. Finally add lemon juice. Before serving, add crushed roasted hazelnuts.

Note: this is a wholesome soup and particularly nice in autumn as all the vegetables are in season.

Escargots Salad Scented with Madeira

Ingredients

A bowl of assorted salad leaves to serve 4
Vinaigrette dressing (see page 33)
24 prepared escargots
2 cloves of garlic, crushed
10ml Madeira
75g butter, cubed
1 shallot, finely diced
Juice of 1/2 lemon
Seasoning

Method: fry garlic and shallot. Add Madeira, lemon juice and escargots and toss lightly in the pan. Whisk in butter and season to taste. Toss salad leaves in vinaigrette, put on a plate and arrange escargots around. Pour hot butter mixture over the finished dish.

Note: escargots are readily available as a number of farms in Ireland now produce good quality escargots.

Gâteau of Clonakilty Black Pudding

serves 4

Black pudding was known at least a thousand years ago, and was probably cut in slices and fried with the breakfast bacon just like nowadays. After a thousand years it surely deserves a facelift. My Gâteau of Clonakilty Black Pudding uses simple ingredients which are easily available, but oh! the difference they make to this lovely honest food. Try it.

Ingredients

16 slices of Clonakilty black pudding
3 large potatoes, peeled
200g mushrooms
1 cooking apple
1 clove of garlic
25g smoked bacon (diced)
50ml pork stock
1 tablespoon of sherry vinegar
Butter for cooking
Black pepper and salt

Method: parboil potatoes and set aside. Cook the apple in a knob of butter without colouring. Sauté mushrooms with sliced garlic. Put apple and mushroom into liquidiser. Purée and set aside. Slice potatoes very thinly and arrange in fan shape (8 fans). Brush with melted butter and season well with salt and milled pepper. Glaze under the grill until golden brown. Fry pudding and smoked bacon in hot pan until crispy. Reheat apple and mushroom. Add a knob of butter and season well.

To assemble dish: using 4 plates, place 1 potato fan on each plate, next a layer of purée, then pudding and finally top with potato fan. Place a small quenelle of mushroom and apple purée on top. Place smoked bacon around the outside the plate. Pour sauce around the finished dish.

Sauce: reduce sherry vinegar by half. Add pork stock (page 29). Season to taste and finally add a knob of butter.

Glazed Galway Oysters with Champagne and Leeks

Ingredients

12 native oysters
2 egg yolks
1 tablespoon of white wine
2 tablespoons of champagne
1 tablespoon of fish stock (see page 26)
25ml fresh cream
^{1}/$_2$ leek cut into fine strips and blanched
1 teaspoon lime juice
1 teaspoon olive oil
Seasoning

Method: wash and open the oysters. Remove from the shell. Put into a pot with champagne, fish stock and juice of lime. Bring to the boil very gently and remove oysters. Set aside. Reduce the juice slightly and add the cream. Reduce again to a heavy consistency. Whisk egg yolks and white wine in a stainless steel bowl over a pot of boiling water until it reaches the ribbon stage to form a sabayon. Add sabayon to the sauce, heat leeks in olive oil and season.

To assemble dish: place leeks in shells with oysters on top and pour sauce over. Glaze under a hot grill until the surface becomes a golden brown.

Note: be careful not to overcook the oysters as they can become tough.

Salad of Salmon with a Tomato and Cucumber Dressing

serves 4

Ingredients

A bowl of assorted salad leaves – iceberg, lollo rosso, curly endive, Chinese leaves, etc
Vinaigrette dressing (see page 33)
¹/₂ cucumber peeled, diced and deseeded
2 tomatoes peeled, diced and deseeded
1 tablespoon of chopped chives
1 teaspoon of lemon juice
4 tablespoons of olive oil
2 tablespoons of fish stock (see page 26)
500g wild salmon
Seasoning (salt and black milled pepper)

Method: toss salad leaves in vinaigrette. Cook salmon in hot non-stick pan and cook to desired taste. Remove and place around the salad. Put fish stock and lemon juice in the pan, reduce slightly and add olive oil, tomato, cucumber and chives. Season well with salt and black milled pepper. Pour dressing around the salad.

Note: here in Ireland we are very lucky to have such good quality wild salmon. Hopefully this will always be the situation. This recipe is ideal for a summer lunch.

Deirdre, Michael and Paddy Kennedy sitting behind
Sirloin of Beef Crusted with Peppercorns and Fresh
Herbs [see p. 55].

Clifford's Gourmet Irish Stew [see p. 69].

Gâteau of Clonakilty Black Pudding [see p. 46].

Poached Free Range Egg on a Bed of Spinach Served
with Nuts and Grapes [see p. 36].

Grilled Fillet of Turbot on a bed of Braised Fennel and
Onion [see p. 64].

A Warm Smoked Haddock Salad [see p. 39].

Pancakes with Summer Fruits [see p. 78].

Caramelised Peaches with Honey and Lavender Ice-cream [see p. 79].

Hamburger of Rabbit on a Purée of White Vegetables

8 mini hamburgers

Ingredients

500g rabbit meat (finely minced)
1 egg
1 large shallot (finely diced)
1 tablespoon of chopped herbs (chervil and tarragon)
Salt and milled pepper
Dash of worcester sauce
1 teaspoon of brandy
500g white vegetable purée, (see page 73)
1 knob of butter

Method: put the rabbit meat in a bowl. Sweat off the shallot with a knob of butter. Add to the rabbit meat with the remainder of ingredients excluding white vegetable purée. Season to taste. Shape neatly into 8 mini hamburgers. Sauté in hot pan with knob of butter and cook to desired degree. Place white vegetable purée in centre of plate. Place hamburgers neatly on top.

Note: these hamburgers are delicious as a starter or a main course. A mustard sauce accompanies this dish very well.

Chicken Quenelles with Milleens Cheese

serves 4

I strongly recommend serving Irish cheeses – which are fabulous – at the end of a meal. But you can also use them inventively in cooking as I have done in my Chicken Quenelles with Milleens Cheese. I love Milleens, which cooks to a perfect consistency and is admirable for this dish. It is made in West Cork by Veronica Steele, a most dedicated cheesemaker. Be warned! Put on a music tape, take the phone off the hook and disconnect the doorbell for Quenelles demand a strong arm, a fine but resistant sieve, and endless patience.

Ingredients

250g chicken breasts
300ml fresh cream
1 egg white
25g Milleens cheese (diced)
Lemon juice
Salt and pepper to taste
Chicken stock for poaching (see page 27)

Sauce

15g Milleens cheese finely diced
250ml chicken stock (see page 27)
100ml white wine
1 small shallot (diced)
150ml fresh cream
1 knob butter
Salt and pepper

Method: put chicken breast in liquidiser. Add egg white and 100mls of cream. Remove and pass through a sieve. Put into a bowl (stainless steel) over ice. Add remaining cream and lemon juice and season. Place in fridge to rest for ¹/₂ hour. Using 2 dessertspoons, form into egg shape quenelles. With a small spoon, place a small piece of Milleens cheese in centre of quenelle. Continue in that way until mixture is used up. Put in shallow dish and cover with hot chicken stock. Simmer in oven (120°C) until the quenelles are firm.

For the sauce: sweat off the shallot with a knob of butter. Add white wine and chicken stock and reduce by half. Add cream and reduce to a light consistency. Whisk in Milleens cheese and pass through a fine sieve. Correct seasoning. Assemble quenelles on a large plate and pour the sauce around.

Note: to complement the quenelles it is nice to make a shape of a hen in puff pastry and then place it on the quenelles and garnish with chopped chives.

Cream of Spinach Soup with Baby Ravioli Filled with Irish Cheese

yields 1 litre

Ingredients

1½ litre chicken stock (see page 27)
250ml cream
25g beurre manié (see page 93)
Seasoning

Spinach Butter

50g butter
75g leaf spinach

Baby Ravioli

24 small 'raviolis' filled with Irish cheddar cheese (see page 88)

Method: cream butter in the processor, add leaf spinach and liquidise again until fully mixed. Put into fridge until required. Reduce chicken stock to ²/₃ initial volume, and add cream. Bring to the boil and whisk in beurre manié. Season to taste. Whisk in spinach butter and serve. Before serving, reheat baby ravioli and place in soup cups.

Note: this soup has proved to be one of the most popular soups on our menu. It is important to note that the spinach butter can be frozen and held for up to 3 weeks in the freezer.

Main Courses

Layered Chicken and Filo Pastry with Fried Bananas

serves 2

Ingredients

2 medium sized chicken breasts
4 discs of filo pastry
1 banana
1 knob of butter
Lemon juice
15g melted butter

Sauce

25ml fresh cream
15ml white wine
15ml port
15ml chicken stock (see page 27)
Salt and pepper
1 shallot finely diced

Method: panfry chicken breasts in knob of butter and carve. Place filo pastry on baking tray. Brush with melted butter and bake in hot oven until golden brown – approximately 2 minutes. Slice banana and fry in butter and lemon juice. Assemble dish by placing 1 filo pastry disc on the plate and then the sliced chicken and bananas and top with second filo pastry disc to complete the finished dish.

Sauce: reduce port, white wine, chicken stock, cream and shallot to a required consistency. Season with salt and pepper. Put sauce around the dish to cover the base of the plate.

Note: if you could buy free range chicken, it would give this recipe even more flavour. It is an easy recipe and very quick to assemble.

Sirloin of Beef Crusted with Peppercorns and Fresh Herbs

Ingredients

1 kg sirloin of beef
1 knob of butter
1 clove of garlic, pressed
40g of assorted chopped herbs (eg, tarragon, parsley, chervil and thyme)
15g of assorted crushed peppercorns – black, white and pink
Salt and black milled pepper

Method: seal beef in hot pan and cook in oven until cooked to desired taste. Combine garlic, herbs, butter and peppercorns and place on top of cooked sirloin. Return to the oven for a further 2 minutes until butter has melted and peppercorns and fresh herbs have crusted. Remove and serve.

Note: a good rich sauce will complement this dish (page 28). When buying beef from your butcher, make sure that the beef is well aged.

Sea Bream Cooked in a Vegetable Stock

serves 2

Ingredients

2 fillets of sea bream (bones and skin removed)
1 shallot
¹/₂ carrot
¹/₂ stick of celery
¹/₄ leek
1 bay leaf
1 sprig of lemon thyme
12 white peppercorns (crushed)
1 sprig of coriander
1 sprig of dill
1 tablespoon of chopped chives for garnish
¹/₂ teaspoon of sea salt
150ml fish stock (see page 26)
25ml hazelnut oil
1 teaspoon of lemon juice

Method: finely chop the vegetables and put into a pan. Add remaining ingredients except for oil, chives and bream and cook for about 10 minutes. Add sea bream to the pan and simmer gently for about 10 minutes. Add chives and oil. Season and serve immediately.

Note: a tossed salad and boiled potatoes will accompany this dish very well.

Escalope of Wild Salmon in a Sea Urchin and Chive Butter Sauce

Ingredients

4 pieces of wild Irish salmon weighing 150g each
4 fresh sea urchins
100ml lemon butter sauce, (see page 31)
1 tablespoon chopped chives
Salt and pepper to taste

Method: prepare sea urchin. Do this by opening the sea urchin and remove juice and meat and set aside. Season salmon and cook in a non stick pan for 2 minutes approximately on each side. Heat lemon butter sauce and add sea urchin meat, juice, and chives. Do not boil sauce. Place escalope of salmon on a plate and pour sauce around.

Note: it is important to use wild salmon where possible. This dish should be cooked at the last minute before serving.

A Fillet of Veal with a Kiwi and Gin Sauce

serves 2

Ingredients

2 x 200g veal fillets

Marinade Ingredients

2 tablespoons of olive oil
1 clove of garlic
1 sprig of rosemary and thyme
1 tablespoon of white wine
6 crushed peppercorns

Sauce Ingredients

1 kiwi (diced)
1 tablespoon of Cork Dry gin
100ml veal stock (see page 29)
6 green peppercorns in brine
Seasoning
1 knob of butter

Method: marinate veal in marinade ingredients for approximately 1 hour. Panfry veal on both sides in oil for approximately 4 minutes each side. Remove from the pan and set aside. Put gin in the saucepan along with kiwi and peppercorns and bring to the boil. Add veal stock and simmer for 1–2 minutes. Pass through a fine sieve. Season to taste and add the knob of butter.

Note: pork can be substituted instead of veal. This is one of my favourite sauces.

Roast Mallard with a Sauce of Locally Grown Figs

serves 2

Ingredients

1 mallard, hung, cleaned and plucked
1 clove of garlic
1 sprig of thyme
2 shallots
1 small carrot
2 figs
1 tablespoon of Armagnac
50g butter
100ml game stock (see page 30)
Seasoning

Method: season the mallard and lightly brown in a hot oven proof pan. Add vegetables, garlic and thyme and place in hot oven for approximately 40 minutes. Make sure while the mallard is cooking that you baste intermittently.

Sauce Method: peel and purée one of the figs and reserve the other one for garnish. Put the game stock in a small pot with Armagnac. Boil, and add fig purée. Cook for 1–2 minutes and pass through a fine sieve. Season to taste. Whisk in butter. To assemble dish, cut off breast and legs of mallard, place legs neatly on the plate, carve breast and put on the plate also. Pour sauce around and garnish with slices of fig.

Note: the bones of the mallard can be chopped and added to the basic game stock to enhance the flavour of the mallard.

Leek and Cheese Flan

Ingredients

300g wholemeal shortcrust pastry
2 large leeks
25g butter
Large pinch of cayenne pepper
3 eggs (free range if possible)
75ml of milk
75ml sour cream
Large pinch of salt
175g grated cheese (Irish cheddar)

Ingredients for wholemeal shortcrust pastry

200g wholemeal flour
2 teaspoons of baking powder
100g butter
2 tablespoons of water

Method: roll out the pastry and use it to line a 23cm flan tin. Cook blind for 10 minutes. Slice the leeks and clean them thoroughly. In a pan, melt the butter and fry the leeks until tender. Season well with cayenne and nutmeg. Leave to one side to cool. Meanwhile, in a large bowl, whisk the eggs, cream, milk and salt together. Sprinkle half the grated cheese over the pastry base. Arrange the leeks on top and sprinkle with the remaining cheese. Pour the egg mixture into the flan case. Bake in the oven at 200⁰C for about 20 minutes until risen and golden. This flan can be served hot or cold.

Pastry: put flour and baking powder in a mixing bowl. Rub in butter until mixture resembles fine bread-crumbs. Add sufficient water to give a soft but manageable dough.

Note: this is an ideal vegetarian dish.

Wood Pigeon and Mushrooms in Puff Pastry

serves 4

Ingredients

200g wood pigeon (breast cut into strips)
1 small potato
2 shallots (sliced)
25g butter
1 clove of garlic (crushed)
2 sprigs of thyme (chopped)
100g button mushrooms (sliced)
50ml cream
200g puff pastry
Salt and pepper to taste
1 egg for egg wash

Method: fry shallot and garlic in butter and add thyme. Cut potato into fine strips and put in bowl with wood pigeon and mushrooms. Add shallot and garlic to the mixture and season. Roll out half the puff pastry to cover the plate (approximately 20cm in diameter). Roll out remaining puff pastry for covering. Egg wash the base and put mixture in the centre. Place pastry cover on the top and seal well with a knife. Cut a slit in the middle. Cook for 15–20 minutes approximately at 175°C. When cooked remove from the oven. Reduce cream slightly until you achieve a sauce consistency. Pour cream into the slit and cook for a further 15 minutes.

Note: rabbit, venison and mallard can be substituted for pigeon. This recipe can be used for either a starter or a main course.

Lambs Liver and Kidney on a Purée of Garden Peas Scented with Orange and Redcurrants

serves 4

Ingredients

4 slices of lambs liver
3 lambs kidneys
150g fresh peas (cooked and puréed)
1 tablespoon of cream
50g butter
1 orange
50g redcurrants
Olive oil for cooking
Salt and pepper to taste
2 tablespoons of dry Vermouth

Method: prepare kidneys by cutting into 1cm pieces. Segment orange and reserve segments for garnish. Reserve pulp and juice also. Reheat the pea purée with cream and half the butter. Season well. Fry livers and kidneys in a hot pan with the olive oil. Remove from the pan and set aside. Add orange juice, pulp and vermouth to the pan with the redcurrants (reserve some for garnish). Simmer for a few minutes. Pass through a fine sieve. Add the butter and season to taste.

To assemble dish: place purée in centre of plate with the liver on top. Arrange kidneys around the liver and garnish with orange segments and redcurrants. Pour sauce around.

Note: my preference when cooking offal is to cook it slightly pink. However, you can cook it to your own required taste.

Baked Scallops in Pastry

serves 2

Ingredients

8 fresh scallops
150g puff pastry
2 shallots finely diced
2 tablespoons of Vermouth
2 tablespoons of white wine
2 tablespoons of fish stock
1 tablespoon of chopped herbs (chives, chervil and dill)
1 teaspoon of lemon juice
Black milled pepper
100ml basic fish cream sauce (see page 32)
1 egg for egg wash
Pinch of salt

Method: prepare scallops and toss in a bowl with marinade made from herbs, shallots, white wine, Vermouth, lemon juice and fish stock. Season to taste. Place in individual baking shells or if preferred, 1 large baking shell. Cover with puff pastry and brush with egg. Make an incision in the centre and leave for 10 minutes in the fridge. Cook for 12–15 minutes at 160°C. Remove from oven and pour hot fish cream sauce into incision and serve immediately.

Note: make sure you do not overcook the scallops as they become tough. This dish can be used as a starter or a main course.

Grilled Fillet of Turbot on a Bed of Braised Fennel and Onion

serves 2

Ingredients

2 pieces of turbot (approximately 150g each)
2 tablespoons of olive oil
1 knob of butter
1 bulb of fennel (finely sliced)
1/2 onion (finely sliced)
25ml white wine
25ml fish stock (see page 26)
2 sprigs of lemon thyme
Season to taste with salt and pepper

Method: dry turbot well. Season and brush with a little olive oil. Place on a hot grill pan. Sear until well marked. Cook fennel and onion in remaining olive oil and butter until transparent. Add white wine, fish stock and lemon thyme. Place turbot on top of vegetables. Cook in oven for 5–7 minutes until fish is cooked. Then assemble.

Note: this dish served with a tossed green salad scented with lemon is very light and flavoursome.

Leg of Lamb with Pear and Thyme Sauce

Ingredients

1 leg of lamb
2 cloves of garlic, sliced
1 pear
1 teaspoon of honey
1 sprig of thyme
1 chopped onion
1 chopped carrot

Sauce

125ml good lamb stock (see page 29)
1 sprig of fresh thyme
4 crushed white peppercorns
1 tablespoon of honey
1 teaspoon of white wine vinegar
1 small pear, peeled and chopped
25g butter
Seasoning

Method: set the oven at gas mark 4, 180⁰C. Prepare the leg of lamb for roasting. Trim, then score the skin. Insert garlic and thyme into the slits. Brush with a little olive oil. Place the joint in the roasting tin with chopped onion and carrot and cook for 1 hour 20 minutes to 1 hour 40 minutes according to taste. A few minutes before lamb is cooked, peel the pear and liquidise or mash with the honey. Remove the joint from the oven and glaze the surface with the honey and pear mixture. Return to the oven and finish cooking. When the lamb is cooked to your liking, wrap in foil and keep warm. Remove the onion and carrot and any excess fat from the roasting tin. Keep remaining juices for the sauce.

To make the Sauce: put all the sauce ingredients except the butter into a saucepan. Cook gently for about 1 minute. Pass through a fine sieve. Return to the saucepan with the juices from the roasting tin.

To serve: carve the lamb. Reheat the sauce, add the butter and quickly stir in. Put a little sauce over each serving of lamb.

Note: lamb is best served in spring. However, it can be served all year round. This is my interpretation of the traditional roast.

Grilled Lamb Cutlets Served with Tomato and Olive Oil Dressing

serves 2

Ingredients

6 lamb cutlets

Marinade

1 tablespoon of olive oil
Sprig of rosemary
1 tablespoon of honey
2 cloves of garlic (sliced)
Sea salt and milled pepper

Method: combine all ingredients together. Add lamb cutlets and marinate for 1 hour in the fridge.

Tomato and Olive Oil Dressing

4 tomatoes, peeled, deseeded and chopped
1 crushed clove of garlic
1 shallot finely diced
1 tablespoon of white wine
1 tablespoon of Dry Martini
4 tablespoons of olive oil
Salt and pepper
$^1/_2$ tablespoon of chopped thyme

Method: fry shallot, garlic and herbs in olive oil. Add tomato, Dry Martini and white wine. Season and set aside. Cook cutlets to desired point. Serve with tomato and olive oil dressing.

Note: this dressing is easy to prepare and can be used for different meat and fish dishes. It makes an attractive lunch or supper dish.

Cork Spiced Beef in a Mango and Ginger Sauce

Spiced beef should not just be served hot with the turkey as a Christmas food. My Spiced Beef in a Mango and Ginger Sauce would grace any table at any time, but especially in summer. The Cork delicacy, Smoked Beef, cut thin when cold, is our replacement for the Italian prosciutto as I think I prove in my recipe serving with Ogen Melon, and a sauce of Sauternes and Passion-fruit: a magnificent, simply prepared and flavoursome first course that will not blunt the appetite.

Ingredients

1kg piece of spiced beef
1 onion
1 carrot
1 stick of celery
1 bunch of herbs tied together
6 juniper berries
6 white peppercorns, crushed

Sauce ingredients

500ml spiced beef cooking juices
1 small mango, mashed
15g fresh root ginger, finely diced
100g unsalted butter

Method: put the spiced beef in the saucepan, cover with water, add vegetables, herbs, juniper berries and peppercorns. Cook gently for approximately 90 minutes.

Method (sauce): pass the cooking juices through a fine sieve. Reduce with the ginger, then add the mashed mango. Season to taste. Whisk in cold butter and remove from heat.

Note: this is a speciality of Cork, traditionally used at Christmas. Now used all year round in my restaurant, as it has proved most popular with my customers.

Clifford's Gourmet Irish Stew

serves 6

The traditional Irish stew was made with mutton. My version substitutes lamb – easier to get nowadays than mutton – softens the flavour with a drop of cream, retains the traditional pearl barley, and adds to the vegetables. Remember that the cabbage must be lightly cooked and not murdered to death! This dish is one of the greatest successes in Cliffords.

Ingredients

1¹/₂ **litres water approximately**
1 leg of lamb (ask the butcher to bone the joint and to chop the bones into small pieces)
2 large carrots
1 large onion chopped
1 small white turnip, chopped
4 potatoes, chopped
1 stick of celery, chopped
50g green cabbage finely shredded and lightly cooked
1 leek finely sliced
100ml cream
Dash of Worcester sauce
Chopped parsley
2 tablespoons of raw pearl barley (soaked and cooked)
Pinch of sea salt and black pepper
Bunch of thyme

Method: cut the lamb into cubes and put in a large pot. Cover with cold water. Bring to the boil. Drain and rinse the lamb, then replace in a clean pot. Add the bones to the pot with thyme, black pepper and salt. Cover with 1¹/₂ litres of cold water. Next add the vegetables but keep aside 1 carrot, the white turnip, 2 potatoes and the green cabbage for later use as a garnish. Cover the pot and cook for approximately 1 hour or until the meat is tender. Remove the meat bones from the pot and discard. Liquidise the cooked vegetables and the liquid. Return to the pot. Add pearl barley, cream and Worcester sauce. Add chopped parsley. Neatly chop and blanch the remaining vegetables. Return the meat and blanched vegetables to the pot. Taste for seasoning. Garnish the stew with cooked shredded cabbage.

Note: this is a modernised version of a traditional recipe and has proved very successful on our menus.

Vegetables

You should never eat vegetables because they are good for you; that way they risk being a medicine, or a penance. Eat them because, properly prepared, they taste incomparable. In Italy, the wonderful vegetables are frequently served as a course on their own (and not just for vegetarians) or make a light and delicate topping for pasta. Our shops are improving their vegetable counters, but still have a long way to go, so search until you find a supplier who understands roots and greenery, and have a till-Death-do-us-part relationship with him and his stall. Or find out in your own garden how many so-called exotics revel in our climate.

Pumpkin Soufflé

serves 6

Ingredients

50g butter
40g flour
250ml milk
3 egg yolks
5 egg whites
Salt
Pinch of paprika
Nutmeg
1lb fresh pumpkin, puréed

Method: melt the butter and mix in the flour to make a roux. Add the milk and stir. Season with a pinch of salt, paprika and nutmeg. Stir over heat until the mixture reaches the consistency of a thick sauce. Remove from the heat and add the purée of pumpkin, egg yolks and gently fold in the egg whites. Butter a soufflé dish and three-quarter fill with the mixture. Bake in a moderate oven 160°C for 17 minutes and serve immediately.

Note: half way during the cooking, it is advisable to loosen the sides of the soufflé. Pumpkin is an unusual vegetable, not used often but makes a nice alternative to other vegetables.

White Vegetable Purée

Ingredients

6 medium sized potatoes
1 medium sized onion
1 parsnip
2 white turnips
25g butter
25ml cream
Seasoning

Method: peel and roughly chop the vegetables and potatoes. Put into a pot and cover with cold water. Cook for 20 minutes approximately until just cooked. Drain well and return to heat to dry out. Purée and whisk in cream and butter. Season to taste.

Note: this is a very versatile vegetable dish, and can accompany many dishes. It is especially good with grilled meats and game.

Aubergine Mousse

Ingredients

500g aubergines (peeled and diced)
¹/₂ litre of cream
5 eggs
1 teaspoon of mixed spice
Salt and pepper
Olive oil for cooking
1 knob of butter

Method: fry aubergines in hot pan with olive oil. Season well with mixed spice. Cook until tender. Purée aubergine in food processor and gradually add eggs and cream and correct seasoning. Pour into buttered ramekins and cook in the bain marie for 10–12 minutes at 120°C.

Note: this is a very tasty mousse and goes well with roast lamb.

Baked Stuffed Potato Dusted with Herb Breadcrumbs

yields 12

Ingredients

6 large baking potatoes
4 shallots finely diced
25g butter
25ml cream
25g chopped chives
25g white bread
25g fine herbs (parsley, chervil, chive and tarragon)

Method: bake potatoes at 180°C for approximately 45 minutes. When cooked, cut each potato across the centre. Remove potato from skins and place in a bowl. Cook the shallot in the butter without colouring. Using a fork, break up the potato and mix in the shallot, butter, chives and cream, and season well. Refill the skins with the mixture. Put bread and herbs into the liquidiser and liquidise until the mixture becomes very fine. Sprinkle crumbs evenly over potatoes and brown under the grill or in the oven.

Note: this is not a complicated recipe, yet it is different and easy to prepare. Can be eaten on its own or makes a pleasant change to serve at a barbeque rather than the heavily used foil-wrapped baked potato.

Vegetable Kebab

My vegetable kebabs make an easily prepared dish for the vegetarians among us, who must be tired of lentils and want something with a festive look. Indeed it makes a great dish for anyone whose system is just tired of meat protein, especially in the summer.

Ingredients

Shallots (parboiled)
Potatoes (parboiled)
Medium sized mushrooms
Small tomatoes
Peppers
Courgettes
Aubergine
Apple
Seasoning

Method: prepare vegetables and trim to required size for even cooking. Thread ingredients carefully on skewers in a colourful arrangement. Marinate in olive oil, herbs and lemon juice if desired for 2 minutes. Season with salt and milled pepper. Cook on hot grill until vegetables are tender.

Note: to complement this dish, creamed spinach may be used. Rest the kebab on the spinach and serve with a lemon butter sauce (see page 31).

Desserts

Pancakes with Summer Fruits

Ingredients

4 pre-cooked pancakes
**A selection of fresh summer fruits to serve 4
persons, ie, strawberries, loganberries, raspberries,
peaches, plums, gooseberries, apples or bananas**
**100ml whipped cream flavoured with 1 tablespoon
of Grand Marnier**
Icing sugar for dusting

Method: fill pancakes with cream. Add the fruit, ar-
ranging it carefully. Then fold the pancake over. Dec-
orate with fresh fruit and leaves of mint. Finally dust
with icing sugar.

Note: to accompany this dish, a purée of raspberries
with stock syrup (page 93) added goes very well. If you
prefer, pastry cream may be used instead of fresh
cream. This is a very simple and easy dessert to prepare.

Carmelised Peaches with Honey and Lavender Ice-Cream

serves 8–10

Ingredients

Ice cream

9 egg yolks
1 egg white
400ml milk
300ml cream
175g sugar
150ml water
2 lavender flowers
2 tablespoons of honey

10 ripe peaches

Caramel Sauce

250g sugar
150ml water
150ml cream
100g butter (unsalted)

Method: make a stock syrup with the water and sugar (page 93). Add the lavender and simmer for 5 minutes. Pass through a sieve and set aside to cool. Whisk egg yolks well, add egg white and then add to the syrup and beat until light and fluffy. Boil milk and cream and add to the mixture. Finally add your honey. Allow to cool and freeze in an ice-cream machine.

Sauce: slice each peach into 8 segments. Set aside. Boil sugar and water in a saucepan and stir until sugar is dissolved. Allow to carmelise until nut brown in colour. Remove from heat and whisk in cubed butter and cream. Add segmented peaches to the sauce and simmer for 2 minutes.

To assemble dessert: put honey and lavender ice-cream in centre of plate. Pour peaches and sauce around. Garnish with fresh mint leaves.

   Note: this is a very luscious dessert not to be indulged in too often!

Raspberry Cheese Cake

serves 6

Ingredients

320ml stock syrup (see page 93)
1 tablespoon of Grand Marnier
300g raspberries
25g praline (see page 93)
170ml whipped cream
2½ leaves of gelatine (soaked in cold water)
2 drops of vanilla essence
Juice of ½ lemon
1 egg
40g icing sugar
1 large wholemeal biscuit to cover base of cheese-cake tin (20cm approximately) (see page 90)
175g cream cheese

Method: cream the cheese with the lemon juice, icing sugar and vanilla essence. Make a sabayon with the egg and Grand Marnier (page 93). Warm the stock syrup, add gelatine and allow to dissolve. Combine the syrup with the sabayon and whisk well. Add this mixture to the creamed cheese. Set aside to cool. Whip the cream and fold into cooled mixture. Pour the mixture into cheese cake tin, which has been lined with the wholemeal biscuit. When set, line the top with fresh raspberries and sprinkle with praline.

Note: raspberries are particularly good with creamed cheese. However, other fruits may be used.

Blackcurrant and Apple Bavarois

Ingredients

2 egg yolks
25g vanilla sugar (sugar with vanilla pod infused)
150ml cream
150ml milk
2 leaves of gelatine
2 eating apples
150g blackcurrants (puréed)
150ml stock syrup (see page 93)

Method: soak gelatine in cold water. Cream egg yolks and vanilla sugar. Boil milk and add to this mixture. Place in heavy pot. Cook over gentle heat until the mixture coats the back of a wooden spoon. Remove from the heat, add gelatine and puréed blackcurrants. Peel and thinly slice apples. Bring stock syrup to the boil. Add apple slices and cook for 1 minute. Whip cream and slowly add to the cooled custard and fruit mix. Line 8 ramekin moulds with the apple slices and pour in the mixture. Put in the fridge to set. For easier removal it is advisable when turning out your bavarois to dip the ramekin first in hot water.

Note: this recipe using apples and blackcurrants is one I use often in the restaurant. The combination of the fruits works wonderfully.

Compôte of Rhubarb with a Muesli Topping

serves 4

Rhubarb is not strictly a native plant, having been brought over from China a couple of centuries ago, for use as a laxative believe it or not. It has made itself a niche throughout the countryside, and there is not a farm without its stand of rhubarb. My rhubarb compôte uses it alongside the real natives known to Fionn MacCumhail – pinhead oatmeal, honey, nuts, butter and wholemeal flour. For an ecologically sound pudding you could not go wrong with this. Put a few wholemeal biscuits beside it on a plate; our Irish wholemeal flour is so good that I believe in making use of it in every possible way.

Ingredients

50g wholemeal flour
50g pinhead oatmeal
1 teaspoon of mixed spice
50g brown sugar
25g chopped, roasted mixed nuts
50g butter
2 teaspoons of honey
100ml water
500g young rhubarb

Method: put honey, water and rhubarb in a pot and poach for 3 minutes. Combine flours, oats, spice, sugar and nuts. Melt butter and mix into ingredients. Put poached rhubarb into dish. Cover with topping and bake in oven for 10 minutes at 165°C.

Warm Pear and Blackberry Pudding

yields 6 puddings

Ingredients

150g blackberries
2 ripe pears
500ml milk
3 eggs
50g vanilla sugar (caster sugar with vanilla pod infused)
200g plain sponge (cut into cubes)
1 teaspoon lemon juice

Method: peel pears and cut into cubes. Sprinkle with lemon juice. Mix eggs and sugar, pour on boiled milk and mix well. Strain through a sieve. Place blackberries, pears and sponge into 6 ramekins. Pour the egg mixture over. Allow to settle for 2 minutes. Bake in a bain marie for 20 minutes at 145^0.

Note: blackberries are not often used. However the hedgerows have an abundance of blackberries which are so tasty and natural. This is why I use this recipe.

Breads

Clifford's Soda Bread

Our native Irish soda bread cannot be improved on in its lovely simplicity. The recipe I give here is for the kind made from white flour, not made quite as often as the wholemeal brown variety but well worth trying. There are however other native foods which can be modernised and (dare I say it?) improved.

Ingredients

500g cream flour
$^1/_2$ teaspoon of bread soda
$^1/_2$ teaspoon of salt
300ml buttermilk
25g butter
1 egg
25g sugar

Method: sieve the flour, salt and bread soda into a bowl. Rub in the butter and sugar, then combine the egg and buttermilk. Add to the flour mixture and softly shape into a cake. Make a cross on top. Cook at 165ºC for 45 minutes.

Clifford's Brown Bread

Ingredients

500g brown flour
25g wheatgerm
20g wheat bran
25g butter
25g sunflower seeds
1 tablespoon brown sugar
1 tablespoon bread soda
1 egg
500 ml buttermilk
1 pinch salt

Method: combine all dry ingredients and rub in the butter. Mix egg and milk together. Add to the mixture. Put mixture into tin and cook for 60 minutes at 165°C.

Note: everybody has their own recipe for brown bread. I use this one as most of my customers are always asking for the recipe so here you are!

Basic Pasta Dough

Ingredients

500g strong flour
3 eggs
8 egg yolks
1 tablespoon of olive oil
Pinch of salt

Method: sieve flour. Mix in eggs and oil. Season and knead to a smooth dough. Rest in fridge before use.

Note: this pasta can be used for ravioli, tagliatelle, or any other pasta dishes (cut and shape to required size).

Although there are a lot of egg yolks in this recipe, the whites can be used to make a large Pavlova filled with fresh fruit and cream.

Banana and Walnut Bread

Ingredients

100g walnuts
250g ripe bananas, mashed
250g caster sugar
1 pinch of salt
2 eggs
250g self-raising flour
30ml olive oil
10g baking powder
65ml milk

Method: cream mashed bananas and sugar in a mixing bowl. Add eggs, crushed walnuts, baking powder, flour, salt. olive oil and milk. Put into a greased loaf-tin. Cook at 160ºC for 40-45 minutes.

Note: to enhance appearance, some sliced banana and 1 tablespoon of brown sugar with crushed walnuts can be sprinkled on top of the loaf before cooking. When cool, dust with icing sugar.

Crunchy Wholemeal Biscuits

Sometimes we just don't have the patience to make breads and patisserie. However this recipe for Crunchy Wholemeal Biscuits is easy and very healthy and well worth the effort. Give it a try.

Ingredients

225g plain flour
225g wholemeal flour
150g brown sugar
50g icing sugar
200g butter
1 whole egg
1 egg yolk

Method: combine flours, brown sugar and icing sugar. Rub in butter and bind with egg. Rest in the fridge for 30 minutes. Roll out the mix to approximately 1/2 cm thick and cut to desired size. Cook in oven for 12 minutes at 160°C.

Brown Yeast Buns

yields 25 buns

Ingredients

454g strong flour
454g wholemeal flour
30g fresh yeast
35g brown sugar
2¹/₂ tablespoons of salt
¹/₂ litre warm water
1 egg for egg wash

Method: mix flours and salt. Combine yeast, water and brown sugar. Add to the mix. Beat with dough hook for a few minutes. Place in bowl and cover with a damp cloth and leave to prove for 40 minutes (approximately) until it doubles in size. Then, knead again and cut into 50g size pieces and roll into balls. Place on floured baking tray and brush with egg wash. Leave to prove for another 20 minutes in a warm place. Bake at 165⁰C for 23 minutes.

Note: various toppings can be sprinkled on the top of the rolls before cooking to enhance, ie, sesame seeds, poppy seeds or oatflakes.

Glossary

Stock Syrup

A combination of sugar and water.

This makes about 1 1/2 pints of stock syrup:

454g caster sugar
568ml water

Dissolve the sugar in the water. Bring to the boil slowly making sure all the sugar has dissolved. Continue to boil the syrup for 1 minute. Cool and store in a jar.

Sabayon

Yolks of eggs and a little liquid cooked until creamy.

Beurre Manié

A mixture of butter and flour used for thickening sauces or soups.

Praline

A selection of nuts set in caramel and then crushed for use.

Bain Marie

A baking tray with a little water used for cooking delicate dishes.

Quenelles

Mousse or purée of meat, fish or vegetables moulded into oval pieces.

Parboil

Partly cooked in salted boiling water.

Sweat

To cook in butter or oil without colouring.

Sauté

To cook quickly in a hot frying pan.

Roux

A thickening of cooked flour and fat.

Ramekin

Oven proof, earthenware dish/mould.

Reduce

Term used when reducing stocks or sauces to achieve the desired consistency.